The ~~Art~~ *Heart* of Buying & Selling Real Estate

Tips and Strategies to Make
Your Real Estate Journey Easier

BY RIAZ AHMED
AND AYESHA SYED

The Heart of Buying & Selling Real Estate: Tips and Strategies to Make Your Real Estate Journey Easier Copyright © 2018 by Riaz Ahmed and Ayesha Syed.

Disclaimer: Although the authors and publisher of this book have made every effort to ensure that the information in this book was correct at press time, the authors and publisher do not assume and hereby disclaim any liability to any party for any loss, damage, or disruption caused by errors or omissions, whether such errors or omissions result from negligence, accident, or any other cause.

The authors have tried to recreate events, locales and conversations from memory. In order to maintain anonymity, in some instances they have changed the names of individuals, places, identifying characteristics and details such as physical properties, occupations and places of residence. Any resemblance to actual persons, living or dead, or actual events is purely coincidental.

The purpose of this book is to educate and entertain the reader. This book is not intended as a substitute for legal advice. The reader should consult the appropriate legal, accounting, or other professionals relating to his/her real estate transactions.

For information contact www.bestgtaagent.com

Published by Prominence Publishing www.prominencepublishing.com

ISBN: 978-1-988925-29-5

First Edition: December 2018

"Ninety percent of all millionaires become so through owning real estate."
~Andrew Carnegie

CONTENTS

Acknowledgments

We are so grateful to all our clients that have given us the opportunity to let us help them in their real estate journeys. We are successful because you put your trust in us to make a difference in your lives. It gives us immense pleasure that we have helped you all with your dream homes and investments and have added value to your lives now and to your financial future as well.

"This is a real-estate-driven economy from top to bottom."

~Christopher Thornberg

What People Are Saying About Riaz & Ayesha

"Riaz and Ayesha provided excellent service. They were knowledgeable, professional, polite and easy to work with. They made the sale of our home a successful and enjoyable experience. Would definitely use them again. Riaz and Ayesha offered us great advice with the timing and pricing of our listing. The marketing of the house, including the professional photos, looked incredible. Their negotiating skills were great. All of this helped us to get a great return on our house in a very short time. We would recommend Riaz and Ayesha to anyone considering buying or selling!"

– Ajay Gupta

"When it comes to negotiations, Riaz and Ayesha are the best! Their understanding of the market and communication is unmatched! Thank you for your hard work and keeping me informed every step of the way."

–A. Farooqui

"Riaz and Ayesha sold our home in seven days! We got out of our house and purchased a home in the community where we wanted to be. I know many people that haven't had that kind of success. Thanks again for everything! We really look forward to having you as a resource and being able to refer friends to you for real estate advice."

–A. Mir

"We had the misfortune of putting our house on the market, because of a requirement to move, just as the decline in house sales in Mississauga began. After a lot of frustration, disappointment, and I believe missed opportunities with another agent, we contacted Riaz and Ayesha. There is a huge difference in the skills, strategies and work ethic required to sell a home in a challenging market from those required in a normal or hot market. I only wish we had found them sooner because they possess the talent needed. Our house sold for a price that made us happy. I do not believe it would have occurred without Riaz and Ayesha."

–K. Khan

"Riaz is an impressive agent. We would gladly recommend him to anybody who wants to sell quickly and for a good price. He takes good care of his customers."

–Aman P.

"I made the mistake of hiring a friend of the family to sell our house. After it sat on the market for over 90 days, we canceled the listing. One of our friends had worked with Riaz and Ayesha and had success, so we decided to sell with them. Three weeks on the market and we had an acceptable offer. We had a smooth transaction and the home even closed one day early!"

–M.A. Iqbal

"Riaz helped me purchase my first home and I have been very pleased with his services. What I liked most was that he always provided his honest opinion and let us make the decision in our own time."

– Ali Razvi

"Riaz and Ayesha did an incredible job in helping me with my investment property. They were very helpful and knowledgeable in all aspects. I would recommend their services to anyone looking to buy a home or investment property."

–Faraz T.

"Riaz did a great job for us when we decided to sell our house. A nice, friendly agent, he's always helpful and hard-working. He kept bringing buyers by until he found the right one. Thanks a lot."

–Ehab Allam

"We bought a home in Mississauga with the help of Riaz. He was very patient and never pressured us as we had very specific requirements for our home. He showed us a lot of properties over a couple of weeks meeting our requirements and finally we were able to find our dream home and have been extremely happy with our decision. We will definitely use

Riaz's services when we need to sell and upgrade our current home."

– Mohammad

"Mr. Riaz Ahmed helped us to purchase our first home and we are so grateful for all his expertise and for taking the time to understand what we needed in a home and guiding us to the best choices."

–Arif Baig

"Riaz Ahmed was an amazing Realtor, his professional attitude towards real estate & detailed knowledge of the current market was spot on and incredible. He helped me get the best price for my home & made me feel special & valued as a client. I'm glad I had him as my realtor & I'll definitely refer to my friends, colleagues & family members."

– Adeel Siddiqui

Preface

I magine there are four home owners whose homes are all appraised at the same amount.

Amira's home sells within 3 weeks of listing for a higher than listing price.

Scott priced his home 5% higher than Amira's home and he sold it in 4 months. However, it sold for $10,000 less than Amira's house.

Jamil priced his home 5% higher than Scott's home and sold it in about 6 months for the same price as Scott.

Maria decided to try to sell her home by herself. One year later, when she had become very desperate, she finally accepted an offer from someone for 15% less than Amira.

◇

The stories above are stories that we hear every day in our business. When homes are listed for sale, some sellers get above average results, and some sellers get below average results, whereas most home sellers get average results.

Obviously, when people sell their homes, they want the most money and they want to sell it as quickly as possible and with very little stress. Amira in the above example was the only one that experienced that result.

◇

Average Realtors get average results. You want to make sure you hire an experienced Realtor with a long history of getting exceptional results for their clients.

Even when a Realtor earns a "Realtor of the Year" award, that could simply mean that they listed the most homes out of all other Realtors that year... but how many did they sell? How many of those listings expired? How many sold at or above the asking price?

How you choose your Realtor is crucial. Do not get awestruck by a high number of listings. It's better to list your home with someone who may have fewer listings but who has a proven track record of selling each listing on the first attempt.

Who would you rather hire: Someone who had 200 listings last year but only sold 56% while the others all expired? Or a Realtor who had 20 listings last year, with 96% of them selling on the first attempt?

Of those two Realtors, who do you think would be most recommended?

Similarly, if you hire a Realtor that has a history of getting average results for their clients, you can be assured that's what you'll get too. Therefore, choosing the right agent is the first step in real estate success, whether you are selling or buying.

Introduction

"We are not salespeople. We are consultants who guide our clients and treat them like they are our family."

~ Riaz Ahmed

R eal estate has always been in my blood. My family is involved in business and real estate in various parts of the world, so it was only natural for me to turn to a career in real estate. Equally important was the concept of my wife Ayesha and I, working as a team, helping other families. Helping families is what we do best because we understand their needs and wants. We treat each family as if they are our own family members and we make sure that they are protected and taken care of during their entire journey of buying or selling their home.

We know how emotional and sometimes difficult it can be when you are selling your home. We know how hard it can be and we feel your pain. It's our job to educate and guide our clients so that they can make the best decisions for their family.

Each family that we work with has their own family dynamics. Depending on the age of their children, we help them decide on what kind of home to buy and which location would suit them best.

For example, if they have young children, we would suggest a nice quiet street, so the kids can play outside and the parents need not worry about traffic and noise. We would also advise them to buy a home close to the school that their children will be attending so that they can walk to school when the time comes.

If a family has college-age kids, their family dynamics will be different, and their needs will be different too. Perhaps the kids will be coming home on weekends and possibly bringing their friends. There should be adequate space for extra people.

We have three children ourselves, so we can relate to the families that we work with.

Ayesha plays a wonderful role when we work together with families. During the sometimes stressful moments, as problems or challenges come up and we are working on overcoming those together, Ayesha helps the family not be affected by that and to remain calm and confident throughout the process. Additionally, there are two of us and our clients have told us that it's always better to have more than one person. Ayesha handles the technical details and marketing and she is the person who is reassuring and lets everybody know that we are on their side.

There are many ways that we help families buy and sell real estate and, in this book, we are going to provide tips, strategies and guidance on how you can make the most out of your next real estate transaction.

"To give real service, you must add something that cannot be bought or measured with money, and that is sincerity and integrity."

–Douglas Adams

1

Why We Love Working With Families

"It takes a family to understand the real struggles of another."

~Ayesha Syed

When we work with families, we often become lifelong friends with them. We treat each family as if they are our own family, and we tend to get quite close to them. We like to stay in touch with them as the years pass and we enjoy seeing their kids growing up.

We have many fond memories of the families we have worked with, but some stand out for us more than others.

Ahmed's Story

Ahmed had an adult child that was handicapped. Because Ahmed was receiving subsidized care from the city, he had a very specific geographic restriction in which to buy his house. As a result of that funding, he had to buy in the Peel Region; his budget was limited and he needed a home that didn't have any steps at the front door or the back yard so his son could enter and exit easily. He also wanted a bigger back yard so his son could spend some time outside. In addition, the backyard had to be wheelchair accessible. To further complicate things, he did not have the entire down payment yet for the house he was going to buy. His credit was somewhat blemished from a past divorce and he was renting a townhome. However, he did have good income to support this purchase as he had been working for a well-known company for a very long time.

We thought and thought about this situation. We not only had a challenge here with the structure of the house, but he also needed about a year to come up with a full down payment and his credit needed time to heal.

When we have clients that need about a year or so to purchase a home but want to get started sooner, we feel that getting into new construction is the best route to take. In this case, Ahmed was going to get helped in several ways. Firstly, with a new construction home, he was getting about nine months to a year to pay the down payment. In the meantime, his credit would have time for the blemishes to fall off. Besides, he would lock in today's price and when his home closed a year later, he would already have built-in equity. Once we got that established, we told Ahmed about it. He was very excited about this idea and was ready to proceed. Now we had to find him a project that was offering homes with a walk-up porch and a big walk-out back yard that would be accessible for his son.

We took Ahmed to several new development projects in Mississauga and Brampton where he was eligible to buy. After an exhaustive search which included visiting the sales centres of several projects with him after work and on the weekends, we found a project in Brampton that was offering the exact home he was looking for. However, there was a big challenge. The builder wanted a deposit of $40,000 in 90 days! Ahmed only had $15,000 at the time. We quickly started brainstorming for a solution. We knew for sure that he needed more time; he was making enough money to save the rest of the deposit but it would take time. We asked Ahmed how much money he could spare monthly after his expenses. He told us he could spare $2,500 every month from his and his wife's income combined. As we had a great relationship with the builder, we talked to the sales manager and told him the situation and how this was going to be the perfect home for his family and son with special needs. We told the manager he could pay $15,000 now and for the next 10 months he could pay $2,500 every month. The manager escalated this to his executive team and in a couple days we received news of the approval.

Ahmed and his family were very happy because:

1. They found the perfect house which matched their requirements

2. Although they were okay with an old home, we got them into a brand-new home

3. We negotiated a down payment schedule that no one thought could be possible

4. They were able to remain in the same area and continue to receive funding for their son.

Result: It's been a year since Ahmed and his wife closed on their brand new house and his home has already gone up $135,000 in value from the day he booked it two years ago. At his one-year check-up we visited him and showed him recent sales in his area that prove the increase in value. He told us that he and his family were so happy that we helped them find their dream home with all the challenges they had. Now, they have become more than clients to us. They are dear friends now and they have since referred many friends and family to us.

Busy Parents of Three Young Kids

We once had a client that had 6-month old twins and a 6-year-old boy. This couple had just relocated from the USA. They were already very overwhelmed with their new responsibilities with the twins and the move had left them both exhausted and drained - physically and emotionally. We all know how difficult it can be to manage with babies, but twins are twice the work, and especially challenging when there's no family nearby to provide support. Of course, they could not just focus on the twins; they had to be sure to support their 6-year-old as well. In this case, the

6-year-old was starting school in a new environment, was also overwhelmed and probably neglected in some ways at home because mommy and daddy were busy taking care of his baby siblings.

This couple was renting a home in Lisgar, a neighbourhood in Mississauga where the school bus for the 6-year old picked up kids at the end of the road which was about 300 metres away. It was winter time and snowing. It was the first time for them to experience Canada's winter. The challenge was that the child was not old enough to walk to the bus stop himself and mom had to walk him which meant that she had to bring the twin babies. Instead of having time with mom in the morning, the older child had to take care of himself because mom was so busy bundling up the babies in order to walk the 300 metres to the bus stop. It was pretty miserable. The dad couldn't help because he had to leave for work early.

For a couple of months (until they found their 6-year old a walking buddy or a parent that would walk him), it became increasingly harder for mom to manage the morning situation. Once she had to drop her child off at school when he missed the bus, and she said that after she got the kids ready and put them in their car seats she was sweating. In winter. She even left the coffee cup on top of the car while doing so and drove off to find it lying in the driveway when she returned.

When we met this couple, their most important requirements were as follows:

- Either the school bus stop be very close to the

house or the school should be inside of 500 metres from the house

- The house should be on a quiet street with at least one bedroom on the main floor

- Close to a park for the kids

- Close to a clinic and pharmacy as the husband was working long hours and mom had to take care of the family.

We then sat down and did some research. We knew that they could afford an average priced house in an upcoming neighbourhood. We did research on schools in different neighbourhoods and bus stops, and a comparative market analysis on homes in their vicinity for amenities - especially the clinic and pharmacy.

Result: After showing them houses for several weeks, we found them a very nice property in Brampton on a quiet street that they could call home. To their amazement, the school bus stop was right in front of the house! The park was about 200 metres from the house and pharmacy and walk-in clinic were walking distance across the street along with the newly built Cassie Campbell Community Centre with lots of activities for kids and adults. This house had 2 living rooms and they decided to convert one into a room where the kids could play so they didn't have to climb the stairs every time to check on the kids. In addition, only two streets away there was a wonderful home daycare where the mom could enroll the kids if she decided to go back to work in the future.

When we went back for the one-year visit, we found out that mom had gone back to work, and she was using the home daycare for the twins. The kids were doing great there and had become very social. Their older child was a lot more connected and the couple was doing great financially and emotionally. They were so happy, and we were so proud of ourselves to help them the way we did. We became very close with them.

Five years later, they bought a business in Missisauga which is about half an hour away from Brampton but during rush hour and in the winter storms it can take over an hour. Now their challenge was their long commute that was draining them and taking time away from the kids. They called us. This time they needed our help to sell their house and help them buy one close to their business. They also needed an elementary school for the little ones but the home also had to be close to a middle school for their older child. We knew that they were in for some serious market education both for their existing home and for the home they were going to buy. They were now both sellers and buyers. In the last five years, so much had happened in their neighbourhood such as new developments both residential and commercial, new schools, parks and other amenities which had driven the prices up in the neighbourhood quite a bit. We knew they would be really happy to know this as they were relying on the funds from the sale of their house to buy the next one because they had spent their savings on the business.

We met them in our office for a market education session about the neighbourhood in Mississauga they were going to buy in. It is important that the sellers know beforehand where they will go after they sell their house and we want them to take their time finding their dream home with the right education and expectations so they don't have to rush and get into just any house because their house sold first. We are consultants to our clients. We are not agents that push their clients to buy something fast without proper research and contemplation of their needs and desires. We help them decide what's best for them. At the meeting we showed them what exists in the neighbourhoods closest to their business. We explored East Credit, Churchill Meadows and Meadowvale areas. First, we worked with their price range to see what and where they could buy in that range.

This is an important step because sometimes what buyers want and what they can afford are two different things. If buyers want a certain type of house that is out of their price range they can get frustrated by what you are showing them if that's what fits their budget. We also showed them homes that fit their requirements but were a little over the price range they had in mind. These homes were in the East Credit area and had better appreciation statistics, so that meant that if they bought their next home there, that it would increase in value better than in the other areas. It was closer to the Square One area where their business was located, as well as schools, parks, Heartland Towne Centre, where there are hundreds of brand name outlets, and every amenity you could ever need.

After the showings, we took them back to the office and sat down to reflect on the properties we had seen. It was clear to them that for the kind of house they wanted to buy they would have to increase their budget by about $50,000 which works out to a couple hundred dollars a month. After looking at the equity they had in their existing house, they concluded that they could safely make this move.

We showed them homes for a few weeks and eventually we found exactly the right one for them. It completely matched what they had in mind We knew that the best way to make sure they get this house is to request the seller's agent to meet our clients with his sellers at the property so we could present the offer in person. This helps sellers and buyers build rapport and settle at a reasonable price and finalize the deal. Our meeting went on for about 3 hours because both families had common acquaintances from their country of origin which they discovered that night but regardless, the negotiation process was fierce. Needless to say, after a lot of countering back and forth, they finally settled at a negotiable price, closing date and deposit. The deal got finalized.

Now we had to sell their house in Brampton. We decided to meet them at their house the next day for a market education in their existing neighbourhood. We researched their neighbourhood beforehand for the price range, the age of the neighbourhood, and what had sold in the last 90 to 120 days. When we educated them on the market analysis, we were able to agree on a reasonable listing price for their home.

In order to sell it fast and for more money, we need to keep in mind how the house shows from the outside (curb appeal) as well as how it shows inside. In the last 5 years, the house had gone through some wear and tear and we needed to address the inside and outside of the home.

On the outside, the landscaping needed some work, the driveway needed to be repaired, and the garage door and front door needed to be repainted. Regarding the interior of the home, most people know that the kitchen is the most important part of the house. Having a clean, bright and welcoming kitchen solves half the equation. Any extra clutter that we have on the countertops, and in drawers and cabinets must be packed away temporarily to make it look bigger and brighter. Any fridge magnets and the things they hold should be removed. This gives a very clean and neutral look for the buyers. A professionally cleaned kitchen also speaks for itself.

They had 3 sofas in the living room so we suggested they remove one and put it in storage to open up the space. We also had them remove personal pictures, awards and other wall art to create a neutral space for the new buyers to picture their own art and furniture in the house. They hired a contractor and fixed the curb appeal and took care of all the changes needed inside of the house in a matter of a week. With these changes, their house was ready to be showcased on the market. We got our photographer and graphic design team to do the following:

1. Take professional pictures

2. Create a virtual tour

3. Design 4-fold robust brochures

4. Design 'Just Listed' postcards

5. Upload the virtual tour to YouTube

6. Advertise online on high traffic sites

7. Advertise on our Facebook page

8. Design ads for print media

9. Send a mass e-mail to our database

10. Create 'Open House' signs

Our assistants arranged the installation of the 'For Sale' sign posts in their yard and got the 'Just Listed' postcards sent out to the neighbourhood. First, we invited just the neighbours to come to the open house on Saturday and Sunday afternoons from 11 to 1 pm. Then we opened for the general public from 2 to 4 pm until sold.

Several days before the house came on the market, we advertised it as 'Coming Soon' which piqued a lot of interest in the house. On the day of the open house, we placed 20 'Open House' signs in the whole neighbourhood all the way to the major intersections. We had a huge response from these activities and also from the internet advertising.

Result: Within a few days we had an offer on the house and it sold over asking price!

2

Helping First-Time Home Buyers

"Now, one thing I tell everyone is learn about real estate. Repeat after me: real estate provides the highest returns, the greatest values and the least risk."
~Armstrong Williams

We really enjoy working with first-time home buyers. It is so thrilling to be able to help them into their first home!

There are four important steps to working with first-time home buyers. They are: education, needs/wants, contracts, and following up.

Education

The first thing we do is hold a meeting to educate them on each step of the process. This helps them feel comfortable and confident with us as their educators and guides. It is our goal to make every transaction as stress-free as possible. Moving is one of the biggest stressors in a person's life and we are there to make it as easy as possible. First-time home buyers are usually nervous and they don't know what to expect, so we educate our clients every step of the way so they can relax and know that everything is taken care of.

Needs vs. Wants

During the meeting, we ask them about their needs and their wants. Many times, we help them understand the difference between the two and realize what they can realistically afford. If they haven't already arranged financing, at this time we help them connect with a lender. Some people have been thinking about their Dream Home for many years, and when the time finally comes to buy their first home, there is a stark difference between what they want and what they need. We explain to them that your first home is not always your forever home. It is usually a stepping stone to get to a bigger home in a few years.

Stoney Creek Clients

We had clients that were pre-approved for $450,000 but their lender told them that they couldn't go over this amount or they wouldn't qualify for a mortgage. We had a meeting with them and discussed their requirements. Since they had young kids and the husband worked from home, they weren't bound to live in any particular area.

They wanted to buy a detached home with a two-car garage. We did our research and told them that Stoney Creek, Hamilton and a few other cities to the West (which were up and coming) would meet their requirements and budget. They agreed and we started looking at homes.

We ran into a problem: Every week they changed their minds about what they wanted as a result of visiting friends in other towns. They would get swayed by homes over there and ask to see homes in those areas. In Mississauga and Oakville, the homes cost $250,000 more. They became too ambitious and unrealistic.

They kept wanting us to show them homes there. They asked us to place low ball offers on a couple of homes and they were disappointed that they were rejected. They kept looking for months until we had to tell them to come to the office for a meeting so we could discuss their requirements again to see how we could help them.

We told them that prices in Stoney Creek had already risen since they started looking. They could have had equity built by now had they bought their home months ago. We also told them that this is the reality and you will have to either change your criteria, location or increase your price range. They couldn't increase the price range and their criteria would only be met in the right location. When we made them aware of this, we were able to help them make a decision according to their circumstances and not what they were seeing in their friends' neighbourhoods. They finally understood.

Result: We were then able to get them into a house they could easily afford, and it met their criteria wonderfully. They later told us that this was the best decision they made because six months later, they were expecting a baby and the wife had to take some time off from work and they could still comfortably afford the house on one income and were glad they didn't go over their budget.

Contracts

The contract is generally the most intimidating aspect for a first-home buyer. After all, there is a lot of money at stake! After we have finished negotiating the very best deal for our clients, then we fill out the contract and present it to the seller's agent.

We always sit down with our clients and review the contract line by line to ensure that they completely understand every aspect of the contract. There is a lot of complex terminology that first-time home buyers have probably never seen before and we need to ensure that they are comfortable and they completely understand everything. We do not want them to sign anything that they do not understand.

When a seller comes back with a counter offer, we sit down again with our clients and explain what it means and ask them if they are willing to agree to the revised terms. Sometimes people get emotionally involved and it's our job to remain calm and see the "big picture." Depending on the circumstances, we might even advise they walk away from a counter offer, especially if it means going over budget.

Following Up

Following up with our first-time home buyers is one of the most enjoyable parts of our business. There is nothing like the feeling of gratitude and excitement that we have for our new home buyers. To know that they have trusted us to help them on this special journey is wonderful.

We always follow up with our home buyers and bring them a house warming gift. When they move in, we make sure they are fed lunch or dinner depending on what time they are moving in. We take them food and drinks, and of course some snacks for the little ones. A couple of weeks later we go to their home with a nice decoration piece for their house and a little gift for the kids. We usually know of a corner or a wall that can house a nice picture or lamp or sculpture that will look great. We continue to visit them every year to see how they are doing. We also stay in constant connection via quarterly phone calls and regular informational e-mails.

Finding the Right House

One of the most important things that we strive to do is listen to our clients. It's so important to really listen to their needs and wants. Then we can match our clients with the right property, one that will serve them best. We always let them take their time; we do not want them to feel rushed.

Sometimes, when a potential buyer comes to us and they are looking for a house that is too expensive for their budget, we have to help them figure out what would be a good fit. If they haven't done their homework, they don't really know what to expect. Sometimes they don't even know if the kind of house they are looking for exists. We have to research what is out there, assess the price according to location, then determine how much home they want and how much home they can afford.

There is a process of really helping them understand how they can have a dream but also how to make it affordable and realistic for them.

What we do with the first-time home buyer is we take them to 6 or 7 houses. Some of them might be $500,000 and some might be $600,000. We say, "Okay, this is a $500,000 house, that is what you can afford. This, on the other hand, is a $600,000 house. We know you want a $600,000 house... but right now in your situation, you cannot afford one."

We give them a history of the market. We show them various houses and then we come back to the office and we talk about the houses that we saw – what they liked and what they can afford. It's very informative for them.

They usually say, "Yes, I know you are right, I think we have to go around $500,000. The other houses at $600,000 are over budget and we cannot afford it." That's so much better than us saying, "You cannot have this." We do not push them to buy whatever we are suggesting, but we educate them by proving to them what they can afford and what fits their needs right now.

Biggest Mistakes

The biggest mistake that buyers make when looking for their home is that they choose the wrong agent. The second biggest mistake is that they choose the wrong location. If they fall in love with a home that is too far away from work, for example, that can be a very difficult and stressful situation.

If they buy with their emotions, sometimes they realize too late that they paid too much for a house. You must have an experienced agent who has been working in the business full-time, day-in and day-out. Your Realtor should not be a family member because there is a line between business and family. When you have a family member Realtor, you might feel like you cannot ask them certain questions, and they may be uncomfortable discussing your finances. You have to have a Realtor who has been in the business for a long time, who has a background in marketing and real estate so they know exactly what you need and how to help you achieve your goals.

Sometimes people get in the hands of agents who only do a couple of deals throughout the year and when they are ready to place an offer, this person just quickly does the paperwork and gets it signed and just doesn't really educate them or tell them "this house is priced $20,000 more; there is another one right down the street that is better because the basement is finished; if you would like to see that one we can arrange it for you." The majority of real estate agents are good people with good intentions. But most are average people getting average results, which can cost a homeowner thousands of dollars.

First-time buyers need to be aware of all the expenses that are involved in buying a house. It's not just the down payment that you need to come up with; there are lawyer fees, mortgage fees, and there is always the land transfer tax. Besides the down-payment, they have to have roughly 1.5% of the purchase price put aside for everything else. Also, if they don't have at least 15% of the purchase price for their down payment, then there is an additional fee that gets added to the mortgage.

We take extra care to educate our first home buyers so that there are no surprises.

We also educate our first-home buyers on all the different geographical areas around the GTA. In some areas, the prices don't increase very much; they would have to wait at least five years for their home value to increase by 10%. Whereas in other areas, even if you buy a little condo or a small townhome, you might get a 10% increase in a year and a half or two years.

We make it our business to study the Market Watch, which is a report distributed by the Toronto Real Estate Board. We study it and then we summarize it for our clients. We can tell according to the type of home and in certain cities, how many sold and what was the percentage of the price going up or down.

We can tell our clients with authority that if you buy a town home for $550,000 and there is a comparable semi-detached for $600,000 then you should go for the semi-detached because that will increase 12% (for example) in a year and a half or two years whereas a town home will increase only 8% or 9%. A $50,000 difference in mortgage is only going to cost you approximately $12-$15 per month extra on a competitive interest rate.

It helps them to see that increasing the purchase price by $50,000 and having more profit down the road is better for them in the long run. An inexperienced agent might not be able to educate them in this way which could lead them to purchase a home that might not be as profitable for them in the long run.

New Construction

We help many people buy new construction homes. This means that they purchase a home before it is even built. For example, in 2014, we helped one of our clients buy a townhouse for $525,000. They moved in two years later when it was ready, on May 19th, 2016. Now the purchase price in that area is around $700,000.

We really enjoy helping people find the right property to invest. In the 2-3 years it takes to build the project, the market increases so much that they more than often get a very well built-in equity by the time they move in.

In the future, if they stay there and, if they ever need to make repairs or renovations far down the road, they have that built in equity.

Also, when you buy a brand-new house, you get a five-year warranty. You have a roof warranty, brand new appliances, and so on so you don't have to worry about anything for 5 or 10 years with a brand-new house.

We also inform our clients in that period where they have the warranty, if they make any structural changes to the house, the warranty will no longer be valid. A lot of people don't know that, and they go ahead and build a new bathroom or tear down the closet; because they have made a structural change, the warranty is void. If they are going to sell it within the warranty period, and they had not made any changes, the warranty would get transferred to the new owner. In this case it wouldn't. The new owner may not want to buy the house without a warranty and therefore they may have difficulty selling the house.

One of our clients called one day and said, "Riaz I received an email from you saying that you have a new project. Can you show me?" So I took him to the project and he really liked it. He said, "Ok, I would like to book this unit," to which I replied, "Sure, no problem. The down payment is $20,000 now and then $30,000." And he told me he didn't have the $20,000. I said, "You have two choices –

you can borrow from someone, use a line of credit or you can ask your mom and dad." He said, "I have neither option available to me." I said, "Okay, so let's give it some thought and get together in a couple of days to talk about it." Two days later, he called me and he asked me to come to his condominium. He said "Riaz, we want to buy a house in this new project and how can we do that? We don't have any money for the down payment." He continued, "We own this condo, can you sell this?" I cautioned him that that would be a very risky move because his condo could be hard to sell. If it doesn't sell right away and if anything happens, he wouldn't get the house. He insisted on listing his condo so we put it on the market and lo and behold we sold it right away.

We went to the builder and negotiated an extension before the booking. When you book a new home you normally have to pay $5,000 initially, and then every 30 days you have to make another payment.

Result: We have good relationships with the builders here so they agreed to extend his payment plan after we told them that the buyer is selling his condo and the down payment is dependent on that. He had the initial $5,000 and then after that they extended it 90 days. Since we sold his condo in 20 days, the closing took place in the next 60-70 days, and in that time he had the money to pay for the down payment. It all worked out perfectly.

3

Mindset Matters

"Whether you think you can or you can't...

you're right"

~Henry Ford

A yesha always says that like in any walk of life, a positive mindset plays a huge role in successful real estate transactions. If our clients are open to it, we also give them guidance on how having a positive mindset can help them in their search for the perfect home. Ayesha knows how to write out affirmations that work. She has done extensive research in this area. Writing affirmations the way the sub-conscious mind accepts them is important for a change to happen in your mindset. Many of our clients love listening to her when she speaks so eloquently on this subject. They even ask her to write some good ones for them with regards to not only for finding their dream home but for other areas of their lives too.

We believe that having the right mindset helps us get favourable outcomes in whatever we are pursuing. When we are positive and optimistic about getting or doing something, we create positive energy around us and with positive energy we can achieve a lot.

When we have clients that are looking to buy or sell their homes, we like to see them with lots of optimism and trust that everything will turn out fine. When we go on listing appointments, we like to take mini sold signs to give to our clients so they can see them all the time and feel the energy of having this sold sign in their front yard.

We also like to help them weed out any mindset blocks that may be preventing them from being optimistic about their situation. Sometimes selling one's home can be quite a difficult process. We help our clients through this time by showing them how to write affirmations or declarations.

These affirmations are soft signals that help slowly embed what you're affirming into your sub-conscious mind and what embeds there takes place. Similarly, when we have buyers that are having difficulty finding what they are looking for either because they have strict requirements or they don't quite know what they want – despite all our efforts and market education – they can't seem to settle down, we also help them with affirmations.

Here is an example of an affirmation we recently gave to a client who ended up finding their ideal home:

"I have found the exact home with the right price and location, where all my dreams will come true and where I will be blessed with abundance, love, health and prosperity."

Rick and Pam came to us with a maximum budget of $525,000. They were looking for their first home and they had a specific community they wanted to be in. This was challenging because every single home in that area was worth over $600,000.

Many Realtors would have said, "That's not possible." But we believe that there is always a way and we began searching for their Dream Home. Ayesha developed affirmations for them and taught them how to re-program their mindset to find their Dream Home. And it worked!

Result: Within 3 weeks, we found them their absolute Dream Home for $517,000! It was in their ideal neighbourhood, and under budget. They were thrilled. What's even more thrilling is the fact that their neighbour's house sold for $565,000 within the next month, so now the value of their house has increased as well.

4

Helping For Sale By Owners

"If you think it's expensive to hire a professional to do the job, wait until you hire an amateur."

~Red Adair

W ell meaning people sometimes try to sell their home themselves because they think it will save them money. These are called For Sale By Owner properties, or FSBO for short. FSBO's are not listed on the Multiple Listing Service (MLS) as they are sold privately which means the owners lose their opportunity to promote their property to thousands of potential buyers. Selling a home by oneself almost always causes enormous stress and anxiety for the sellers for several reasons.

First, most Realtors won't take their clients to see a

FSBO property as most often it doesn't offer a commission to them. This sounds harsh but it's true. The FSBO house misses out on thousands of potential buyers.

Second, potential buyers don't know if the owner will act according to the law, like a Realtor is ethically bound to do. How does the potential buyer know if the owner has disclosed a leaky roof or a basement that has once flooded?

Third, because the owner doesn't have the marketing power and reach of a Realtor, the house usually sits on the market for months and potential buyers begin to think there is something wrong with the house.

For these reasons, we love to take FSBOs out of their misery and sell their homes quickly and for a higher price than what they would have gotten on their own. This way they have peace of mind and they know someone is taking care of the laws and policies for them. Besides, their Realtor can negotiate a higher selling price and other terms that work in favour of the seller. This way the Realtor's commission is never a problem when they get more money for their house.

Sold in Two Weeks

Last year we sold a house in Burlington in 7 days with multiple offers. During the open house that we held there, there was a couple who attended and asked for details on the house. Later in the conversation, they disclosed they had been trying to sell their house on the same street for the last month and a half. They were wondering if we had a client we could refer to them from this open house that might like to buy theirs, especially if they were interested in the same area. They also mentioned that they didn't have too much time left as they were relocating. They were selling the house by themselves because they thought they were capable of doing so through advertising on Craigslist and Kijiji.

They were hopeful they would find the right buyer because they only needed that one buyer that would say *Yes*. They thought, "What's the point of paying a real estate agent to do the same and make a commission with little effort?"

We told them that we have expertise in helping FSBO clients and that they needed to know the pros and cons of selling their home by themselves vs. a real estate agent which will help them determine which way they should go. If they felt we could help them, we will be glad to sell their home faster and for more money.

They agreed, and the following week we met at their house. First of all, they had priced their house a little too high and it had therefore become a comparison home. We told them that even real estate agents can't tell you how much your house should be priced at unless they see your home from the inside so sales in the area don't always accurately represent the right range for pricing the home. We told them that most homes on their street had finished basements, pools and a very nice curb appeal. Their house didn't have a pool and the curb appeal needed some work but it had a newly finished basement. Therefore, we needed to price according to its features and do the necessary work in it to showcase it better and then it would sell faster.

They were not marketing it professionally nor taking their phone calls professionally. We told them that the agents on our team have studied scripts that allow them to ask questions to potential buyers that will not only qualify them to buy their house but also give them feedback that they get from showings so they know how they are doing. Furthermore, we would advertise it using the MLS and our proprietary list of marketing tools we have created to effectively market homes for sale. This way thousands of agents with buyers will be able to show their home and they will be able to find a buyer faster and for more money. We told them we would show them how to make it presentable with some repairs, organization and better curb appeal. So, paying our commission would not be an issue because we were confident that we could sell it quickly and for more money.

They had beautiful furniture but needed some adjustments. We advised them to rearrange some of the furniture, and place lamps in areas. Good lighting is essential. In the kitchen, we had them remove everything from the counter tops, put away all the fridge magnets and place a nice flower vase on the island. They also got their home professionally cleaned. We advised them to remove picture frames of family and other personal items from the walls and bedrooms. They removed all extra items from the bedrooms and organized the closets so the space could be appreciated. After that the house was ready for showings. We listed the house and scheduled an open house.

Result: We sold it in two weeks. They were so happy.

The Smallest House on the Street

Mr. and Mrs. Ali were sensitive about their home being the smallest one on the street. For that reason, they didn't think their house would sell fast enough or high enough to justify a Realtor's commission. For six months they tried to sell it themselves but had no luck.

We contacted them one day to see if we could help them sell their home but they were too fixated on the idea that they couldn't sell it for enough profit to pay our commission. We told them that they must have some good equity built into the house and it should yield them good profits after the sale of this home. We also told them that we would give them tips to make their home ready for sale so people won't mind paying more. Then paying our commission would not be an issue. They told us that they had incurred quite some debt in the past years and were looking forward to paying it off after the sale of their home.

We further explained that if they were open to the idea, we could sit down and show them what they needed to do to prepare their home for sale whether they hired us or not. For that we also needed to do a walk-through of the house. They agreed and we met at their home.

We saw that they had a lot more furniture than needed and it was old and not arranged as well as could be. They were baseball fans and they had baseball videos, baseball books and baseball cards all piled up next to the T.V. There were baseball related pictures and souvenirs everywhere in the house. The kitchen had 2 tables – one square and one round – and it was a little too crowded. A few of the light bulbs were fused in the living room. One light fixture had more than a few missing glass pieces. All in all, the house was not presentable to show potential buyers. They agreed they needed to fix a few things but instead of putting more money in the house, they wanted to sell as is.

We made a list of items as we did the walk through and told them all the things that needed to be fixed or removed so we could help them sell for more money and faster. We also crunched some numbers and showed them how much profit they would get from the sale of this house if they sold it themselves without any repairs and without making the house presentable and then compared those figures to selling with us and committing to some repairs and cleaning.

We were positive that they could easily sell the house for an extra $20,000. They were thrilled and agreed to do as we said and hired us.

Their home might have been the smallest but it had a functional layout and was somewhat open concept. We asked them if they would get a storage space for 4 weeks and remove some of the living room furniture and one of the dining tables, as well as all the baseball paraphernalia, pictures and souvenirs. We also told them to replace the light fixtures in the living room and kitchen. We gave them ideas with some pictures of the past work we've done with our clients. We also told them how and where to buy quality but reasonably priced fixtures.

We advised them to paint the living room and hang wallpaper with a modern pattern on one of the living room walls and the bathrooms, which made their house look outstanding. We have several contractors on our team that have done fabulous work for our past clients and they charged them very reasonable rates. They agreed with our recommendations and started preparing their home to sell.

In 10 days, they removed the extra furniture, cleaned the house thoroughly, removed all the extra items, got new bright and beautiful light fixtures installed, got wallpaper hung and got the house painted in neutral colours. We also encouraged them to enhance the curb appeal of the house by getting the porch and stairs washed and by placing a nice new doormat. The house was now very presentable and ready to be put up for sale.

They spent a little money on the house but they knew they would get it all back threefold. We then announced the Open House.

Result: We did 52 showings that weekend with 3 offers and sold it for $25,000 more than the asking price! They were so happy and so relieved.

5

Expired Listings

"Surround yourself only with people who are

going to lift you higher."

~Oprah Winfrey

I t can be very frustrating for a home owner when they have their house listed and it fails to sell during the listing period. This is called an expired listing. We often work with expired listings because we are 100% confident that we can sell their house for them.

We have a formula that we use, and it is very effective. The first thing we do is to visit the home and make a visual inspection, research the neighbourhood, the price range, how old the neighbourhood is and what has sold in the last 90 to 120 days. Then we give our advice on what needs to be changed, repaired, replaced or removed.

We believe the reason listings fail to sell boils down to one thing: Marketing. And if the previous Realtor had priced it wrong, that is also a part of the marketing. Sometimes, the homeowners themselves are at fault if they have not been able to make their house available for showings. But usually it is the fault of the Realtor. You can't simply place a For Sale sign on the front lawn and hope for the best. There is a lot of work that needs to be done to sell a house. That's why when we work with sellers, we have a very detailed plan that we follow.

Hamid's House Couldn't Sell

One of our very good clients Ali referred us to his friend Hamid who had tried to sell his house with another agent but it didn't sell and the listing had expired. Hamid was very frustrated with this situation and couldn't understand why his house failed to sell. Hamid and Ali were good friends so Ali told him to call us if he was serious about selling this house. Ali had mentioned us before but his wife was related to the previous agent so they felt obligated to work with him.

Hamid called us and after we had our initial chat, we got some property information from him and set up the appointment for the next day at 7:00 pm at their home. We asked to make sure both husband and wife would be at the meeting and that it will take at least one hour so they knew what to expect. Before the meeting, we did our research on the neighbourhood, how many homes had sold in the last 90-120 days with the same square footage, if they had a finished basement, and all the same features of their house.

We discovered they lived in a good location, very close to Winston Churchill & Burnhamthorpe in Mississauga but homes in that area are 25-30 years old. After our research, we discovered that many homes in the area had been upgraded, with new roofs and new windows, updated landscaping and other aesthetic improvements.

At the meeting, after a little introduction, we asked them a series of questions:

1. Why do you want to sell?

2. How long have you been living in this house?

3. How much did you pay for it?

4. What is your mortgage balance left?

5. What's the square footage of this house?

6. What upgrades did you do?

7. Did you update the roof?

8. Has the furnace been updated?

9. Were the appliances upgraded?

10. What do you like best about this house?

11. Why didn't the house sell?

12. When are you looking to move? Do you know where you will go after you sell?

13. If your house sells in the next month, where

will you move?

Then we asked them to give us a tour of their house and tell us a little bit about the areas of the house and why they think this will be valuable for the buyer. After the tour, we sat down and started to discuss our findings. The first thing we noticed when we arrived at the house was that their roof was very old and was missing pieces of shingles and needed to either be repaired or replaced. We also noticed that the landscaping lacked appeal.

Inside the house, the light fixtures were very old and some were even rusty, which is definitely a turn off for potential buyers. The living room walls were stained. The kitchen appliances were very old. Knobs on the kitchen cabinets were broken or missing. In the bedrooms, the sliding closet doors were hanging loose or didn't close properly. All closets were jam packed and literally overflowing. Even the bathroom mirror had a crack!

Although it seemed like a lot, we told them that these were simple, but mandatory, tasks they would have to fix to make the house presentable. They agreed, and Hamid said he could take care of everything himself except the roof. We gave him a list of roofers we recommend.

We then installed a 'Coming Soon' sign in their front yard. In about 10 days they got everything on the list accomplished and did not even have to spend very much money at all. Then one of our team members guided them to stage the house. Our photographer came and took pictures and created the virtual tour, our design team designed the whole marketing campaign, and we did Open

Houses on weekends.

At the Open Houses, we had balloons for the kids and for adults we had gift baskets. Our Open House signs were all over the neighborhood. We distributed the 'Just Listed' signs before the Open House and invited the neighbours personally. We advertised in print and internet media. We sent e-mails to our agent database so other agents would know about this property. We also sent an e-mail blast to our client database and did some social media campaigns

Then we helped our clients with some mindset techniques. We usually give them a sticker with the word 'SOLD' on it. It's about 5 inches high and 7 inches wide.

We like our seller clients to look at it every day, all the time and visualize a sold sign on their front yard. They love it and it helps change their energy and choice of words to the positive so they keep focusing on thoughts that their house will sell fast – and it does.

Result: In 2 weeks we sold their house with 2 offers and a little over the selling price.

Being Available For Showings

We once had quite a challenging experience with a family that had to terminate their listing with another agent because they just couldn't keep up with the demands of showings. Our client was a family of 7; husband, wife and 5 kids of which 3 were school going and 2 were toddler twins. The wife, Sara, was a homemaker and the husband, Amin worked a night job for the time being. He had secured a professional job in Montreal and they needed to sell their house within 2 months.

His current night job hours were from 11 p.m. to 7 a.m. When he came home in the morning, the older kids were getting ready to go to school and he was going to bed. His wife's challenge during the day was to handle the twins and keep them quiet while he was sleeping. And she also had to somehow manage to cook and clean and take care of the other household duties while being very quiet.

They listed their house 2 months prior but it didn't sell. The main reason for that was that they didn't know what to expect after their house went on the market. Their agent did not prepare them. Whenever they got a call for showing during the day, the wife had to cancel as her husband was sleeping or because she couldn't keep the house tidy because the twins needed her attention. They secured several evening and weekend showings but eventually, they needed a break and clearly, a better solution. So they terminated the listing. Their previous agent was a part-time sales person and due to lack of experience did not foresee what this family would go through after their house went on the market.

It's an interesting story how we met Amin initially. Amin worked at a gas station in Mississauga near Heartland where I (Riaz) had stopped to get gas. Everywhere I go, I am always very friendly with people and I am almost always dressed in a suit. After a nice chat, Amin asked me what I do for a living. I gave him my card and told him that I am a real estate agent. The next thing you know, poor Amin was telling me all about his situation and all the frustration he had been undergoing. Life was very stressful for Amin and his wife. I told him that I believed Ayesha and I could help them. In fact, we set up an appointment for the next day in the evening to meet him and his wife at their house.

When we met them at their property in Brampton, near the Mount Pleasant Go station, they were very frustrated. They said they had already wasted 2 months and they had only 2 more months left to sell the house and relocate. Their rental property in Montreal was ready and they had already paid the deposit. They needed to sell this house to get the equity so they would have some cash to settle in a new place. They also told us about the trouble they went through managing the showings and how they had to turn down many showings. They felt that the situation was getting out of control and they could not see any way to fix it.

After we let them vent, they felt better and we started to troubleshoot. First, we wanted to find out what time of the day they could show with ease. We had a series of questions to figure out what would be a good time to show. We knew that there had to be about 3 to 4 hours where they could accept showings. So, we asked them all the details of when the kids leave and return, when Amin wakes up in the afternoon and when does Sara get done with her household chores. They told us that the kids arrived from school around 3:00 and Amin also woke up around the same time. Sara got done with household chores by noon. They said that they could leave the house every day around 4:00 because they had to take their kids for tutoring and soccer practices most days of the week. Other days, they said they could go to the library.

So, now that we had that part figured out, we asked them for a tour of their home. Their home was quite nice and clean. It was a newer home so it didn't need any major repairs or fixing. Sara had done a beautiful job with the house. The landscaping needed some attention which could be taken care of in a matter of days. Amin said he had a friend that could take care of it. In fact, he called him right then and asked him to come that evening to take a look.

Before we came over to their house that night, we had done our research of the neighbourhood and we felt that the house was previously priced in a good range but we needed to have a strategy in place to have lots of showings in that 4-hour window every day. We wanted to elicit an overwhelming buyer response.

So, here's what we did. We priced the house $50,000 below market price. We put in the MLS remarks area the following:

- Showings will **only** take place between 4:00 p.m. to 8:00 p.m.

- There will be open house on weekends from 2:00-5:00

- The offer presentation was set to take place on the following Tuesday.

Short and sweet and to the point!

Because of the price, we had over 70 showings, which resulted in 6 offers. There was one perfect buyer that had fallen in love with the house and knew its worth and paid several thousand dollars over the asking price.

Result: We sold the house in 9 days and the family was overjoyed and hugely relieved from the burden of keeping the house clean and leaving the home at 4:00 every day of the week and for open houses for two weekends. Asim and Sara then referred us to Sara's sister Nazia for an investment property and she has since referred several clients to us.

Meriam's Story

Several years ago we had a seller named Meriam who came to us after trying to sell a property for 3 months through another agent. She was having a lot of problems selling her property in the Danforth area because it was occupied by a difficult tenant that wouldn't allow showings to take place. When he did, the place was untidy and dirty. Her agent couldn't do much about the situation and stopped answering the phone after the listing expired.

She was really looking forward to the sale of this property because she had a fair amount of equity built into it and needed cash to put a down payment towards her newly built house in Oakville. She was desperate to sell this property because she didn't have much time left to close on the new property.

We asked her if she had kept the tenant in the loop when she had listed that property the first time. She said she had just told the tenant after the fact and he had agreed to open it for showings after some resistance. We told her that we will have to device a plan to sell this property and we will have to keep the tenant involved in the process because opening it for showings and keeping the house clean will be dependent on the tenant making it happen. She agreed.

We asked her how she felt about getting the house professionally cleaned and having the tenant maintain it so it would be easier for both of them. She thought it was a brilliant idea. We also asked her if we could meet the tenant with her and see if he was open to working with us sell the property. She agreed and we met the tenant. He was a full-time college student and had 2 part-time jobs and just didn't have the time to deal with showings. Otherwise, he was flexible with us in selling the property. For some odd reason Meriam's and her tenant's communication was not clear until then. Meriam hired a cleaning lady to clean the entire unit thoroughly and it looked very nice. We had the tenant agree to put all his shoes inside of the closet rather than leave them all in the foyer and keep his laundry and other personal items tucked away as well.

We then listed the house and we gave Meriam a couple affirmations to write every day.

Here are the affirmations:

"I have found the buyer that has fallen in love with my house and has offered the right price for it just in time for me to have the cash available to close on my Oakville home."

"My tenant is co-operating with showings and keeping the house clean every day."

Result: She diligently wrote her affirmations and we received an offer from an investor after 3 weeks. They closed the deal and gave the tenant the option to stay.

6

Preparing Your Home For Sale

"The way you live in your home and the way

you present your home for sale are two

different things."

—Riaz Ahmed

T he condition of your home has an enormous effect on how quickly your house will sell and how much it will sell for. We always do a walk though of our client's home before listing it, so that we can explain what we believe needs to be repaired or upgraded prior to listing the home.

We understand that sometimes when people need to

sell their homes quickly, they do not want to invest a lot of money into upgrades and repairs. However, it is consistently shown that your house will sell faster and for more money if you do some of the items on the following list. This checklist will provide you with an efficient approach to improving the saleability of your house. Of course, you do not need to do them all! Use it as a guide to check and see what needs to be done.

Major Repairs

These may represent a hefty expense but it's important to take care of major problems ahead of time in order to allow the buyer to feel confident they are making the right choice.

EXTERIOR

☐ Walkway

☐ Steps

☐ Driveway

☐ Siding

☐ Gutters

☐ Downspouts

☐ Roof

☐ Fences

☐ Windows

INTERIOR

☐ Ceilings

☐ Walls

☐ Floors

☐ Paint

☐ Wallpaper

☐ Trim

☐ Furnace

☐ Water Heater

☐ Electrical

☐ Septic

☐ Kitchen counters

☐ Kitchen appliances

Neutralizing

Exterior

Remove the following if possible:

☐ Broken down vehicles

☐ Recreational vehicles (RVs)

- ☐ Boxes
- ☐ Piles of leaves, debris
- ☐ Lawnmower
- ☐ Gardening tools
- ☐ Sports equipment
- ☐ Children's toys

Interior

Remove the following:

- ☐ Fridge magnets
- ☐ Valuables
- ☐ Family mementos
- ☐ Magazines & newspapers
- ☐ Personal photos
- ☐ Knick knacks
- ☐ Offensive teenager décor
- ☐ Awards/trophies
- ☐ Video game items
- ☐ Piles of paperwork

Cleaning & Maintenance

A house that is dirty or smelly will stop a buyer right in their tracks. Prior to putting your home on the market, make sure the following items are operable and in good condition.

Exterior

- ☐ Vegetation (shrubs, trees)

- ☐ Windows

- ☐ Chimney

- ☐ Outdoor lights

- ☐ Garage door

- ☐ Doorbell

- ☐ Interior

- ☐ Walls (no holes or cracks)

- ☐ Handrails are secure

- ☐ Lights – all functioning

- ☐ Fireplace – cleaned by chimneysweep

- ☐ Caulking in kitchen and bathrooms

- ☐ Drains – not clogged or slow

- ☐ Toilets
- ☐ Air conditioner

Major Cleaning

Prepare to do a major cleaning of your home. If you cannot do it yourself, hire professionals. You'll be glad you did.

Exterior

- ☐ Lawn, shrubs, trees, garden
- ☐ Garage doors
- ☐ Front entrance – sweep, clean door and windows

Interior

- ☐ Carpets
- ☐ Hardwood floors
- ☐ Tile floors
- ☐ Curtains
- ☐ Blinds

- ☐ Walls (yes, clean your walls)

- ☐ Windows

- ☐ Mirrors

- ☐ Ceilings (remove cobwebs)

- ☐ Fans and light fixtures

- ☐ Fireplace (clean the brick)

- ☐ Closets (organize)

- ☐ Kitchen (sinks, counters, cabinets, pantry)

- ☐ Furnace (change filter)

- ☐ Air conditioner

- ☐ Attic (they will look here)

- ☐ Basement (of course they will see this too)

When a potential buyer walks into your home, they subconsciously assess it immediately with four of their senses. They smell, see, touch, hear... and maybe during an Open House they might also taste.

The Senses

Consider the following to ensure that a potential buyer

falls in love with your home.

Sound

- ☐ Turn off all TVs

- ☐ Turn off all appliances (some of them give off a slight hum)

- ☐ Ensure you do not have squeaky floors

- ☐ Close windows if there is outside noise

- ☐ Play soft music on the stereo

Sight

- ☐ Make sure your curb appeal is beautiful

- ☐ Place fresh flowers in the home

- ☐ Turn on all the lights inside the home

- ☐ Open all curtains and blinds

- ☐ Light a fire in fireplace

- ☐ Ensure the house is perfectly clean and decluttered

- ☐ All personal items removed

Smell

- ☐ Make sure the rooms smell fresh and clean

- ☐ Put a small dish of light potpourri in the living room

- ☐ Heat water and cinnamon in a pot on the stove

- ☐ Eliminate pet odors

- ☐ Eliminate food odors

- ☐ Eliminate smoke odor

- ☐ Take out the trash & recycling

- ☐ Consider using scented candles

Touch

- ☐ Make sure there is no rough wood on the floors or banisters

- ☐ People like to touch countertops – keep them squeaky clean

- ☐ Ensure that the temperature suits the season – turn on furnace to keep it toasty warm or air conditioning to keep it refreshingly cool

7

Selling Your Home
For Top Dollar

"Success is a state of mind. If you want

success, start thinking of success."

–Dr. Joyce Brothers

I t is obvious that everyone wants to sell their home for top dollar. But in order to do that, we have to be strategic. This is where experience comes into play. People always ask, "How much is my home worth?" and the truth is, it is worth what someone will pay for it. Our job is to find that person, and make sure they fall in love with your home.

There are five main things to keep in mind if you want to

get top dollar for your home. They include: pricing, upkeep and repairs, staging, marketing and hiring the right Realtor.

Pricing

The listing price that you set for your home is a crucial part of the process. If it is priced too low, you're leaving money on the table, and if you price it too high the property will not sell and it will sit on the market for months and months. People might wonder if there is something wrong with the house.

Buyers are very educated these days and they are often looking online for a long time before they even reach out to a real estate agent. Therefore, they are quite savvy about how houses should be priced.

Your Realtor should be able to tell you what price all the similar homes in your area are selling for. Working with an educated and experienced real estate agent plays an important role in your decision to sell your home and creates the possibility of selling it for top dollar. Every real estate agent wants to sell your home for the highest price possible because they will earn a higher commission; unfortunately, sometimes they do not have the experience to know exactly what to do.

Be sure to find a Realtor who listens to you. They must be fully aware of your goals and the true reasons behind why you are selling your house. Sometimes people are selling their house because they are going through a divorce or other major changes in their life, and they must feel comfortable enough to disclose this personal information to their Realtor. That's why we always say that you should never hire a family member as your real estate agent.

Staging

First impressions matter and it's very important that potential buyers fall in love with your home as soon as they see it. You want to make sure that they can envision themselves living in your home. That's why a professional stager is worth their weight in gold. They know enough about real estate to understand who your target market is and who would most likely buy your home. It's not just a matter of hanging some pictures on the wall or substituting a new lamp; professional stagers really know how to make your house have an emotional impact on potential buyers. Study after study has shown that homes which are professionally staged sell more quickly and for more money than homes that are not staged.

Repairs

Make sure that every single thing in your house is functioning perfectly. If there is anything that needs to be repaired do it yourself or hire someone to do it for you.

Nothing turns off a potential buyer more than the feeling that your house is going to be a lot of work. They will likely put in a low offer because they believe that the house is not in move-in ready condition. They also may worry that there are other things wrong with your house that they just can't see. They may wonder, "If the owners neglected to repair this, what else have they neglected?"

By simply repairing everything that needs to be done, you can fetch thousands of dollars more for your home.

Marketing

The better marketing that your real estate agent does, the more people will see your home. You want to hire an agent who is very experienced in marketing because this will mean that you have a larger pool of potential buyers to draw from. Your Realtor will know who the ideal buyer is for your home and should market directly to them using a variety of methods – both online or off-line. When they describe your home, they should be able to paint a picture that makes it very appealing for your ideal buyer.

Every house that we sell is different, so we customize the marketing plan depending on the home's specific features and benefits. Here are just some of the things that we may do when we list your home:

- ☐ Place the for sale sign on the property
- ☐ Enter the listing in the MLS directory
- ☐ Perform a walk-through of the house and offer staging advice
- ☐ Feature the property on our website and blogs
- ☐ Advertise the home in our magazine

- ☐ Set up Internet exposure on over 50 other websites through online syndication
- ☐ Schedule weekend open houses to the public as requested
- ☐ Promote the property in-person at weekly sales meetings
- ☐ Arrange for professional photos and virtual tours
- ☐ Send out direct mail of "Just Listed" postcards to the neighbourhood
- ☐ Create and distribute promotional flyers
- ☐ Install an electronic lock box for easy agent access and security
- ☐ Promote the property on social media
- ☐ Send out email blasts to our list of agents
- ☐ Send out email blast to our list of potential buyers

8

Selling Your Luxury Home

"Luxury must be comfortable.

Otherwise, it's not luxury."

~Coco Chanel

C onsidering the high value of luxury homes, it is understandable that sellers are concerned with getting everything right. Luxury homes are considerable investments, and worth well over a million dollars in our area. Compared to the rest of the market, there are fewer luxury homes available at any given time, which makes it all the more crucial that we position the home correctly.

It's important to attract the right buyer, and make sure that the buyer understands the value of the home. We need to be able to convey what makes each house worth the asking price. Having the correct listing price and an experienced real estate agent are two very important factors in the sale of a luxury home.

Here is what we need to keep in mind when selling a luxury home:

Create a profile of the potential buyer.

Luxury home buyers are obviously a high-end clientele.

With a luxury home sale, it differs from lower priced homes because we are not trying to reach as many 'average' buyers as possible; rather, we are going to market the home to a very specific audience. We cannot take the risk of marketing the home to people who are not qualified to buy it, otherwise that is a waste of everyone's time.

Beyond the customization of the home, the stunning architecture, and the high-end amenities of the property, we also look at where the home is located with regards to schools, restaurants and so on.

The homeowner will have a solid understanding of what separates their home from other luxury properties in the area and the Realtor will market to those strengths. Understanding what motivates a luxury home buyer is imperative.

Price it correctly.

A luxury home has to be priced right from the start. Pricing any home correctly is challenging, so it takes an experienced Realtor to know how to price a luxury home. They need to be able to justify the price and cannot just pull a price out of thin air because it's a unique home.

One of the things that makes it tricky is that there are fewer comparable homes to reference, and each luxury home tends to have unique features that only some buyers will value.

If it is priced too high, and it will sit on the market for ages without selling. Eventually, potential buys will assume there is something wrong with it.

Consider the timing

Luxury homes often have beautiful views. It may be a lake, or expansive views of the city. In winter, the rain and snow may obscure the many benefits of the beautiful view. Obviously, selling such a home would be easier in nicer weather, and the home would most likely sell for more if buyers could see it in the best possible light. If time is not a factor, we'd recommend selling in Spring, Summer or Fall. Here in Toronto, we don't advise selling a luxury home in the middle of winter unless you absolutely have to.

In the spring and summer, buyers can take a stroll around of the grounds which is often a great selling feature in luxury homes. They will see and experience things that you can't appreciate in the winter such as the swimming pool, tennis court, gorgeous flowers and landscaping and possibly other features that might be covered up by snow.

Use effective marketing

Finding the right buyer for a luxury home requires a particular marketing strategy. The way to do so is to advertise online. Simply putting up a listing on the multiple listing service (MLS) is not enough to sell a luxury property – or any home, for that matter as previously mentioned.

Your Realtor should develop a customized marketing plan for your house. You will want to work with someone who has the ability to reach buyers who will want what you are offering. Ask your Realtor how they plan to do this.

The real estate agent you choose to sell your luxury home should have an established online marketing presence and a track record of being able to market luxury homes. Ask to see their previous marketing materials. Will they do online advertising, print ads, or both? Are they knowledgeable in Search Engine Optimization and do they market on Social media as well? People really love looking at luxury properties and fantasizing about owning one. Your Realtor should be experienced in running marketing campaigns to affluent clients.

Use professional, high-end photography and video.

Nowadays, almost all buyers find their dream home online before scheduling a viewing. The fact is that they fall for the pictures of the home first. A luxury home requires very high-end photos. A professional photographer knows how to position everything in the photo just right. They also bring their own lighting to make everything look perfect and inviting. A luxury listing also needs to include a video tour of the home.

Should you have an Open House?

Although we commonly do Open Houses for our sellers, we do not recommend them for luxury homes. Why? Because people are very curious about luxury homes and they want to come just to see the inside of the home. They typically are not even qualified to buy!

An Open House may even attract criminals who are using the Open House as a way of getting in and scoping out the home. Not only is there is a risk of having items stolen, but they can also see what kind of alarm system there is and where the sensors are located.

Instead of a public Open House, we put the house on a Broker tour or do a Broker's Open House. This ensures that all the Realtors in the area know the home is for sale and we can interact with them and ask if they have any potential buyers.

Luxury homes often have features that are not found in any other type of property, such as high-end fixtures, cabinets, appliances, woodwork, and innovative lighting and decor. Luxury home may have some of the following features:

- ✓ High end home theaters
- ✓ Wine cellars
- ✓ Indoor/outdoor pools with exquisite grounds
- ✓ Sophisticated security systems including surveillance cameras
- ✓ Hard wired music system
- ✓ Energy monitoring
- ✓ Wireless control of heat and lights
- ✓ Window covering controls
- ✓ Complete "smart home" capability

Each of these features needs to be understood by the Realtor so he or she can easily explain them to potential buyers if he or she wants to get the best price for the home.

Not every real estate agent is capable of selling luxury real estate.

When you are looking for the best possible service, you need to have an agent that understands luxury home and knows how to sell it to potential buyers. Keep these things in mind when choosing your real estate agent.

9

How to Prepare Your Home for Showings

"Success occurs when opportunity meets

preparation"

~Zig Ziglar

W hen your Realtor tells you that you have a showing scheduled, it's time to get ready!

Make sure your home is perfectly tidy and neat. As soon as you listed your house you should have decluttered and put all personal items away. Now is the time to make sure that there is nothing else laying around. Most importantly, make sure you put away your family calendar so that people visiting your home do not know your schedule. It would not be good for strangers to know when you are going on your family vacation and leaving your home vacant!

Be sure to turn off your computer so no one can access it. Also, make sure all your mail is put away so that they cannot see any of your confidential information. Likewise, medicine needs to be put out of sight because you do not want them to know any personal information about you; for example, they might see your full name printed on the bottle.

Family photos are also important items that you might want to put out of sight. Since you really do not know the potential buyers who are going to be coming into your home, it's best not to let them look at pictures of your family members.

You want to make sure that your house is very bright and clean and welcoming so that potential buyers will come in and really like what they see. Here are some of the things that you should do:

1. Open all the curtains. Make sure the house is very bright by turning on all the lights, even if it's the middle of the day. It is very important to turn on all the lights because if your home is dark people will not feel that it is a welcoming home. Lighted homes sell far more easily than dark homes. Leaving the curtains open allows beautiful natural light to fill the home too.

2. Consider playing some nice, soft music. Background music helps people feel at home and

they tend to stay longer in the home.

3. Consider how hot or cold your home is. You want your visitors to feel comfortable, so you may need to adjust the heat or air conditioning as needed. If it's a hot summers day, you want them to come inside and feel cool and comfortable and relieved that you have a cool home. In winter, you want them to come inside and feel happy to be warm and cozy.

4. Put your pet away. If you have a pet, it can be very challenging for your Realtor to show your home. Even if you have the nicest dog in the world, many people are afraid of dogs and they can make showing your home difficult. If at all possible, remove your dog from your home during showings. Don't just put it in the backyard because then the barking might drive people away and they might be afraid to go into the backyard to take a look around. If you absolutely cannot remove your dog, consider putting your dog in a crate for the duration of the showing.

After your house has been tidied, decluttered, and very well lit with all the lights on and curtains opened, the most important thing for you to do is leave the house. It is crucial that you are not at home while your house is being shown to potential buyers because you want them to feel comfortable in your home and able to ask questions to their Realtor without you listening in.

10

How to Choose a Realtor

"Stop selling. Start helping."

~Zig Ziglar

C hoosing a Realtor to help you buy or sell your home is one of the most important decisions you'll ever make. While some Realtors specialize in selling homes and other Realtors specialize in buying homes (these are called buyer's agents and seller's agents) our team helps people buy and sell homes.

A good real estate agent will help you with the following things:

✓ They will meet with you to see your property and discuss your goals

✓ If you are listing your house, they should provide you with a detailed marketing plan as to how they're going to sell your house.

✓ They should have a marketing strategy to determine and define the asking price

✓ They should help you prepare your property for market including arranging help with decluttering, staging, repairs, painting and anything else required

They should ensure that their marketing is more than enough to expose your home to all the potential ideal buyers.

✓ They must communicate with you on a regular basis and give you progress reports

✓ They must be honest with you when providing feedback

✓ They must have your best interest in mind when negotiating on your half

✓ They must be very organized and make sure that the closing process goes as smoothly as possible

Your job is to make sure that you hire an extraordinary "above average" Realtor if you want above average results. Remember, average Realtors get average results.

The ideal agent is not always the one with the most sales under his or her belt, or the most years on the job. The ideal agent is one who listens to you, is easy to get along with, and has the tools and skills to address your unique situation.

Every home buyer is unique. Some may have credit issues. Some are buying from out of the province. Some need help selling their current home in order to buy a new one. Just as buyers have different needs, real estate agents have different skills and specialties.

Here's how to find the agent who's right for you:

Ask friends & family for referrals

Nobody knows you as well as your friends and family so they are often the best place to start. Very often you will know someone who can recommend an agent who is well-suited for your needs. You can also trust a referral from friends or family more than one that comes from a stranger.

Interview several agents

Statistics show that 84% of home buyers choose the first real estate agent they contact. This means one of two things. Either most people are choosing wisely the first time, or they're just rushing into things without shopping around.

You don't have to exhaust yourself interviewing agent after agent, but at least talk with two or three to see who you're most comfortable with (which leads to the next point).

How do they make you feel?

Experience and credentials are important when choosing a real estate agent, but communication skills are equally important. After all, you'll be working with this person anywhere from 2 to 3 months, so it's important for you to like them and feel like you can trust them. We all have unique personalities, and that's the way it should be. But when working with someone professionally, it helps if their personality matches well with your own.

Ask how they search for homes

When choosing a real estate agent to help you buy a home, ask how they will search for homes. Some agents may have their own particular listings that they favor. But you want what's best for you, not what's best for them. Afterall, you're hiring them to work for you. So make sure the agent that you choose is willing to go above and beyond for you. Are they willing to search high and low to find the best home for you? Will they email you about listing that they find or will they call you? Make sure you let them know how you like to be communicated with.

Always read paperwork carefully

Of course, you know that you will need to read any

listing agreement or purchase agreement carefully. But equally important is the agent agreement. Make sure you understand what you are signing and don't be shy about asking questions. In most cases it's a simple, standard document, but just be sure to read it carefully.

11

Why Trust Matters

"The trust you genuinely and sincerely instill in the first few minutes of your conversation, lasts forever!"

~ Ayesha Syed

Because buying real estate is generally one of the most expensive transactions of a person's lifetime, it is crucial to have trust in your Realtor.

Your Realtor is the person who knows all the laws and rules and regulations better than the buyer or the seller and therefore your realtor has an obligation to make sure that you are protected and taken care of.

A good Realtor is continually educating themselves and keeping up-to-date on the real estate market as well as local by laws and regulations that may affect your real estate transaction.

If you do not trust your Realtor completely, you will not be able to feel comfortable with the decisions that you make. When people trust their Realtor, they refer their family and friends knowing that they will be well taken cared of.

A Realtor that you trust should be able to speak honestly with you. They need to be able to communicate the good news and the bad news to you so that they are delivering correct information. If a potential buyer views your home and has negative feedback, your realtor must convey that information to you and you need to trust their advice.

It's important that your Realtor knows your needs and wants so they can help you responsibly. They will ask you many questions, not because they are trying to be nosy, but so that they can help determine what exactly it is that you need. They need to have truthful information from you so that they can guide you appropriately.

How We Helped a Client Sell One Home and Buy Six

Our client Khalid was moving to the U.S. with his family. He owned a beautiful home in Burlington that he needed to sell. Khalid remembered us because when he was buying this house 5 years ago, our mortgage team had helped him in securing a mortgage on it. A couple of years after that, we had also helped them with two investment properties in new construction in Oakville which turned out to be fabulous investments.

Khalid and his wife, Sophia, called us and told us that they were moving in a couple of months and needed us to take a look at their house and list it for them. We made an appointment for the following weekend and met with them at their house. As usual, at the listing appointment we brought the market analysis of their neighbourhood and according to what had sold there in the last 90 days, and for how much, we priced his home at $789,990. It was a detached home of about 2,500 sq. feet with a double car garage and a finished basement.

They had kept the house in immaculate condition. We listed the house and showings started to take place. Three days later, we received a phone call from a businessman, Abu, that travelled a lot to the Middle East and wanted to buy a house to live in occasionally with similar features as Khalid's house but he wasn't sure of the location and he wanted close to 3,000 sq. ft. We showed him homes in Mississauga and Oakville but he wanted to see more. So, we told him about Khalid's home and the fact that we had listed it 3 days ago but it was only 2,500 sq. ft. He agreed to go see it and he really liked the house. He wanted to place an offer on it and get the inspection done right away so he could leave the next week as planned. We placed the offer, Khalid and Sophia were impressed at how fast we were able to get an offer on the house. They were happy with the price that was offered too because we had educated Abu on the neighbourhood and being a fair and savvy businessman, he knew he was paying the right price for the house.

The inspection was done and everything was fine. The closing date also worked out just in time for them to move to the U.S. Khalid and his family were so pleased with our service and we were so happy to find our own buyer for Khalid's house.

A year later, Khalid and Sophia called us as they had been following the GTA's booming real estate market and wanted to be a part of it again. They told us they were going to visit in a month and buy a couple of properties. We told them we were ready for them. We added them to our email list. This way, they started receiving properties of interest via e-mail and could familiarize themselves with the market beforehand so when we did our market education with them, they would be well aware of what has happened in the past year. When they arrived, we showed them several resale homes and new construction properties in Burlington, Oakville, Stoney Creek and Hamilton. This took us 10 days of relentless hard work from morning to midnight because we needed to prepare the market analysis and compare several projects to make sure they were going to buy the right one.

They decided to buy a stacked townhouse in Burlington near Station West, and two urban townhomes in Stoney Creek for investment purposes. These were going to close two years later and had good deposit payment structures.

Happy with the service they had received so far, they

then wanted us to show them detached homes just like the one they had sold a year earlier. They wanted to have a nice home in the GTA now to lock in the price and if they decided to move back, they would have a place they could call home. Prices in the GTA had skyrocketed and to find a home in Burlington of the same kind they had before was going to cost them upwards of $900,000. So, we had another market education session where we asked them about the price range they were comfortable with and how much down payment they had and after getting them qualified through our mortgage team, we figured they could afford a rather luxury home in Stoney Creek for under $800,000. We started our search and after several days of showings, we found the showstopper! It was an immaculate, over 3,000 sq. ft. fully upgraded home with a big driveway, stone porch, a designer chandelier in the entrance, upgraded light fixtures, motorized window shutters, a huge gourmet kitchen with professional appliances, 4 bedrooms, a backyard with fire pit and gazebo, and a home theatre with surround sound in the basement.

This was truly a dream home and they wanted to place an offer right away. It was being offered for $749,000. We did our market analysis. This home was exceptional because there wasn't another home in the neighbourhood like this one but none of the homes had sold for close to the asking price. Khalid and his wife said they would be comfortable paying $720,000 for it. We felt that there was too much of a gap but we told them that we can offer that much but the offer would most probably be countered close to the asking price.

We placed the offer and lo and behold, they did counter the offer close to asking price and they excluded the gazebo in the backyard which had a value of about $14,000. Riaz then got on the phone with the seller's agent and had a long conversation with him. In this conversation, he had not only negotiated the price to $725,000 but also had them include the gazebo. Khalid and Sophia got the inspection done and signed the contract that night and the deal was firm.

Result: Today, Khalid and Sophia own a beautiful home in Stoney Creek and have several investments under their belt.

Conclusion

As mentioned throughout the book, there are so many important things to consider before buying or selling real estate. We hope that the information we provided herein has been helpful and has answered any questions you may have had.

Whether you are already a homeowner and thinking of selling, or you are just starting out and looking forward to purchasing your first home, we hope that the information provided in this book has helped you.

We always strive to help our clients have a pleasant, satisfying and successful real estate experience and we have proven for many years to go above and beyond the call of duty for them.

Our clients are not just "customers" – they become our cherished lifelong friends.

To your success,

Riaz and Ayesha

About the Authors, Riaz Ahmed & Ayesha Syed

Riaz Ahmed

Direct: 416-825-9730

Email: bestgtaagent@gmail.com

Riaz Ahmed is known for his honest and compassionate approach which helps him serve his clients with sincerity.

Riaz is very knowledgeable about the Mississauga and Brampton markets and is continually studying and constantly learning more with every year that passes.

Riaz has previously worked at fortune 500 companies in the US & Canada in sales and marketing and he has more than 30 years of sales experience.

Riaz's friends, family and clients love his contagious sense of humour.

What makes Riaz such a successful Realtor? As his clients confirm, it's his enthusiasm, energy, and honesty.

Ayesha Syed

Direct: 416-857-9731

Email: bestgtaagent@gmail.com

Ayesha Syed is known for running our real estate practice from behind the scenes. There's so much that happens inside the office simultaneously as the outside field work and she keeps track of our whole team.

Ayesha is very knowledgeable about real estate transactions, the market and the marketing side of real estate. She has also been successfully publishing the 'Real Estate Free Guide' magazine in Mississauga and Brampton since 2011.

She has previously enjoyed a robust career in fortune 500 companies in the US as an Information Technology professional for 15 years as well as taught IT related courses at a community college in Dallas, Tx for 6 years.

What makes Ayesha such a successful real estate agent? As her clients confirm, she's very knowledgeable and resourceful and has the ability to find the exact solutions to her clients' needs.

Checklists

Seller's Checklist

FIND A REAL ESTATE AGENT

- [ ] Hire an experienced agent who knows the market
- [ ] Determine the agent's knowledge of the area
- [ ] Get referrals from family and friends
- [ ] Make sure you can trust your agent and will be comfortable working with them

SET A REASONABLE PRICE

- [ ] Talk to your real estate agent to help you calculate the market value of your home
- [ ] Find simple ways to raise the value on your home
- [ ] Look into how much your neighbours are selling their home for
- [ ] Consider notable features of your home

GET YOUR HOME READY

- [ ] Open all blinds and drapes to keep your home bright and turn on lamps and lights
- [ ] Remove all clutter and keep out of sight
- [ ] Clean and dust the house thoroughly

- ☐ Keep valuables locked up
- ☐ Wash down driveway and patios
- ☐ Put out some softly scented candles
- ☐ de-personalize home

MARKET YOUR HOME

- ☐ Talk to your agent about the best way to market your home in your area, they will know what's best and an experienced agent will take care of this for you
- ☐ Stage your home for bright, clean, and clear photos

PREPARE FOR THE CLOSING

- ☐ Consider and compare offers with your broker
- ☐ Book movers
- ☐ Find a lawyer for closing

Buyer's Checklist

FINDING THE RIGHT HOME

Consider:

- [ ] the location and neighbourhood
- [ ] the size of the property and home
- [ ] the type of home — for example, detached, duplex, row house or condominium
- [ ] the travel distance to work, recreation and services
- [ ] any special features you want or need — for example, accessibility or efficiency upgrades
- [ ] your lifestyle needs and possible changes in the future
- [ ] your preference for a new, resale or custom-built home

FINANCING YOUR HOME

Are you financially ready to own a home? Look into these **5 calculations and questions** before you meet with your broker or lender.

1. Compare how much you currently spend on expenses and debt payments with the amount you have saved or invested.
2. How much can you afford to spend on housing each month without risking your financial health?

3. How much do you need to save to pay for the upfront costs of buying a home?
   Upfront costs include:

   - the down payment
   - home inspection and appraisal fees
   - insurance costs
   - land registration fees
   - prepaid property taxes or utility bills (the buyer reimburses the seller or builder)
   - legal or notary fees
   - potential repairs or renovations
   - moving costs
   - GST/HST/QST on a newly built house or mortgage loan insurance

4. How much would you be spending each month with homeownership expenses added to your current financial situation?
5. What is your credit score? You can demonstrate your ability to consistently pay bills and debts with a copy of your credit report.

WHEN YOU'RE ALL SET

You need to meet with your broker or lender to start the mortgage pre-approval process. Bring the following information to the meeting:

- ☐ government-issued photo ID
- ☐ contact information for your employer
- ☐ proof of address
- ☐ proof of income
- ☐ proof of down payment

☐ proof of savings and investments
☐ details of current debts
☐ your credit score

A pre-approved mortgage tells you:

- how much you can afford
- what your interest rate will be
- how your monthly mortgage payments will look

MAINTAINING YOUR INVESTMENT

Your home is likely your biggest investment. You should plan for the responsibilities of homeownership even before you move.

Consider the following tips for new homeowners:

- **Make your mortgage payments on time.**
  Late or missed payments can lead to extra charges and affect your credit rating.
- **Anticipate the costs of operating a home.**
  Extra expenses may include repair and maintenance costs, snow removal and alarm monitoring.
- **Live within your budget.**
  Check every few months to see if you're spending more than you earn. If you are, find new ways to save more or spend less.
- **Save for emergencies.**
  Set aside 5% of your income as an emergency fund to be ready for unexpected expenses.
- **Protect your home and family.**
  Prepare an emergency evacuation plan and check

fire extinguishers, smoke alarms and carbon
monoxide detectors regularly.

Call Us Today For Your Free
Home Evaluation

416-825-9730